Pebble® Plus

Understanding Differences

Some Kids Are
Deaf

Revised Edition

by Lola M. Schaefer

CAPSTONE PRESS
a capstone imprint

Pebble Plus is published by Capstone Press,
1710 Roe Crest Drive, North Mankato, Minnesota 56003
www.mycapstone.com

**Library of Congress Cataloging-in-Publication Data is
available on the Library of Congress website.**
ISBN 978-1-5435-0997-7 (library binding)
ISBN 978-1-5435-1001-0 (paperback)
ISBN 978-1-5435-1005-8 (ebook pdf)

Editorial Credits
Sarah Bennett, designer; Tracy Cummins, media researcher;
Tori Abraham, production specialist

Photo Credits
Capstone: 12; Capstone Studio: Karon Dubke, 5, 9, 13, 15, 17, 19;
Science Source: Life in View, 11, Spencer Grant, 7; Shutterstock:
adriaticfoto, Cover, Andrey_Popov, 21, DoozyDo, Design
Element

Note to Parents and Teachers

The Understanding Differences set supports national social
studies standards related to individual development and
identity. This book describes and illustrates children who are
deaf. The images support early readers in understanding the
text. The repetition of words and phrases helps early readers
learn new words. This book also introduces early readers to
subject-specific vocabulary words, which are defined in the
Glossary section. Early readers may need assistance to read
some words and to use the Table of Contents, Glossary, Read
More, Internet Sites, Critical Thinking Questions, and Index
sections of the book.

Table of Contents

Deafness

Some kids are deaf.

Kids who are deaf

cannot hear.

Some kids are born deaf.

Other kids become deaf

from a sickness

or from getting hurt.

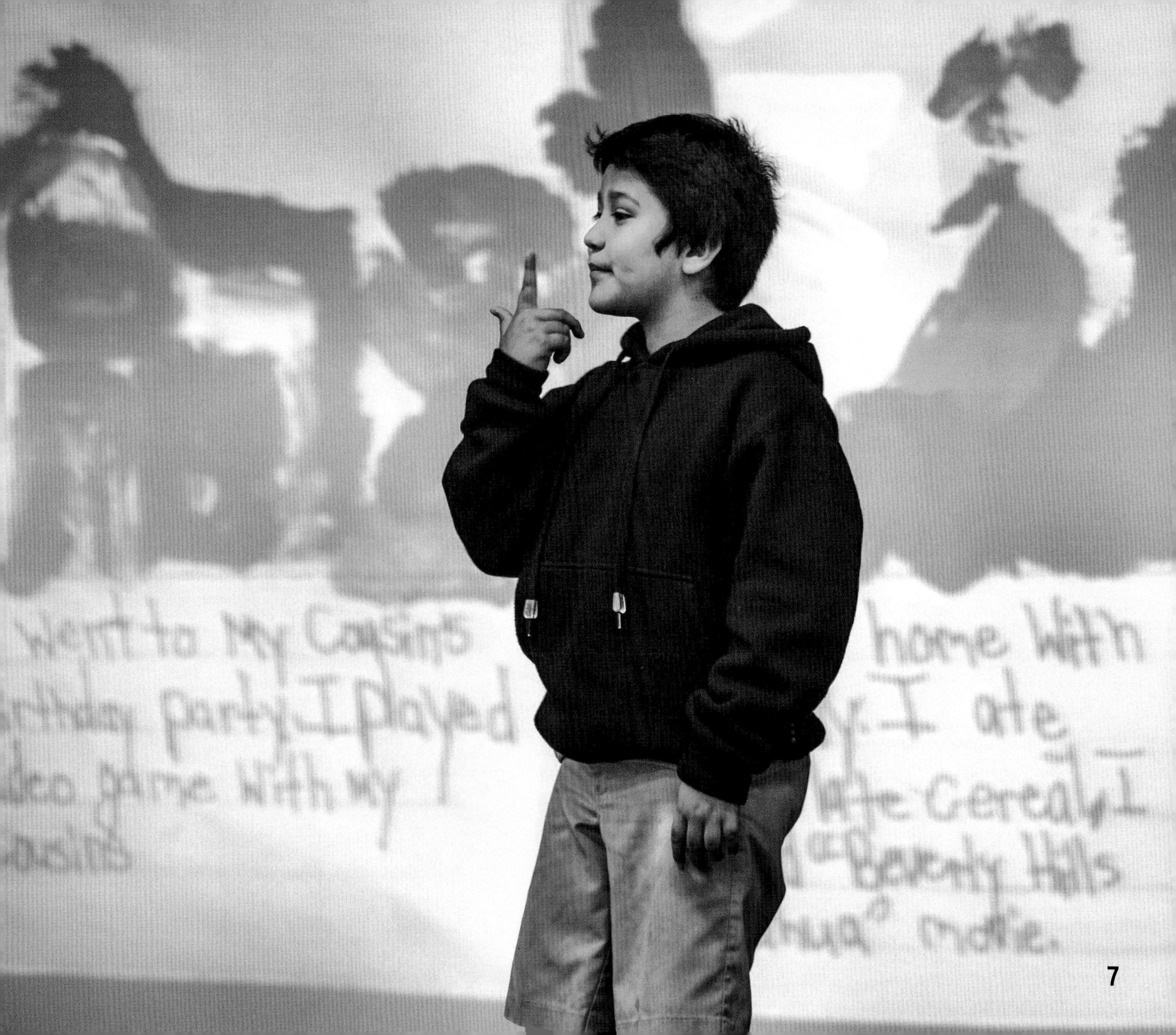
went to my Cousins
home with
party. I played
I ate
game with my
Cereal.
Beverly Hills
movie.

Tools for Hearing

Some kids can hear a little.

They wear hearing aids

to hear sounds louder.

Some kids who are deaf
get cochlear implants.
Implants help them hear
some sounds.

Talking

Some kids who are deaf
use sign language to talk.
Sign language is hand signs
that stand for letters, words,
and numbers.

Sign Language

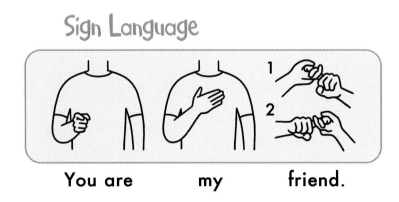

You are   my   friend.

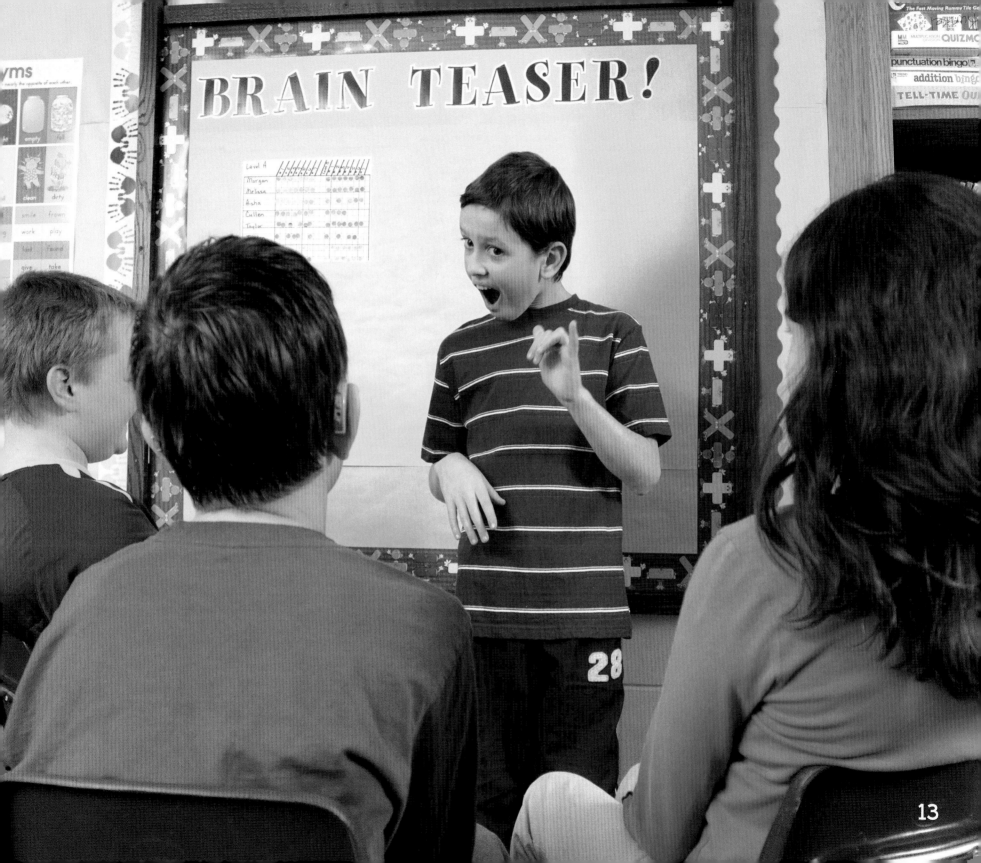

BRAIN TEASER!

Some kids who are deaf
use their voice to talk.
Speech therapists teach
them to speak clearly.

Everyday Life

Kids who are deaf depend
on their sense of sight.
Flashing lights tell them
it's time for class.

Kids who are deaf watch TV
with closed captioning.
The words tell what people
on TV are saying.

TV
G

MACAPA

AMAZON
BASIN

BRAZIL

STRADDLING THE EQUATOR,
MACAPA, BRAZIL IS AN EXOTIC WORLD

ORION

MTS STEREO

Kids who are deaf depend on
their sense of touch.
They can feel a phone
vibrate when a friend sends
a text message.

Glossary

cochlear implant—a small electronic device that is surgically put into a person's head; cochlear implants allow sounds to get to the brain

deaf—being unable to hear

hearing aid—a small electronic device that people wear in or behind one or both ears; hearing aids make sounds louder

senses—ways of learning about your surroundings; hearing, smelling, touching, tasting, and sight are the five senses

sign language—hand signs that stand for words, letters, and numbers

speech therapist—a person who is trained to help people learn to speak clearly

text message—words sent from a cell phone to another person's cell phone

Read More

Clay, Kathryn. *Signing in My World: Sign Language for Kids.* Time to Sign. North Mankato, Minn.: Capstone, 2014.

Kent, Deborah. *What Is It Like to Be Deaf?* Overcoming Barriers. Berkeley Heights, N.J.: Enslow Elementary, 2012.

Internet Sites

Use FactHound to find Internet sites related to this book.

Visit *www.facthound.com*

Just type **9781543509977** and go.

Super-cool stuff! Check out projects, games and lots more at **www.capstonekids.com**

Critical Thinking Questions

1. What other senses are helpful to a person who is deaf?

2. Describe sign language.

3. How do flashing lights at school help children who are deaf?

Index